POEMS

OF

RELIGION AND SOCIETY.

BY

JOHN QUINCY ADAMS,
SIXTH PRESIDENT OF THE UNITED STATES, ETC., ETC.

WITH

Notices of his Life and Character,

BY

JOHN DAVIS AND T. H. BENTON.

NEW YORK:
WILLIAM H. GRAHAM, PUBLISHER.
1848.

828
A214
v.2

Entered according to Act of Congress, in the year 1848, by
WILLIAM H. GRAHAM,
in the Clerk's Office of the District Court for the Southern District of New York.

Stereotyped by BANER & PALMER,
11 Spruce Street.

729

CONTENTS.

PUBLISHER'S NOTICE.

It is known to all the friends of the late ex-President Adams, that it was his custom from early manhood to devote his leisure moments to literature; and the fruits of his literary studies, when collected in an appropriate form, will show that he is entitled to high consideration among our authors. Among his poems are a translation * of Wieland's "Oberon" that has never been published. His "Dermot McMorrogh" failed of a just appreciation, on account of his political relations. Many of his minor pieces have wit, humor, grace, and tenderness, and they are all informed with wisdom and various learning. Some of his "hymns" are among the finest devotional lyrics in our lan guage.

This collection of Mr. Adams' shorter poems is, of course, incomplete, having been made from the periodicals and miscellanies in which they were originally printed; but the editor has made it as perfect as his opportunities allowed, and he is confident that, in the absence of any other volume of the same kind, he has done an acceptable service to the reading public.

New York, Sept., 1848.

* See Griswold's "Prose writers of America," Article J. Q. Adams

SKETCH

OF THE

LIFE OF MR. ADAMS.

BY THE HON. JOHN DAVIS.

JOHN QUINCY ADAMS was born in the then Province of Massachusetts, while she was girding herself for the great Revolutionary struggle which was then before her. His parentage is too well known to need even an allusion; yet I may be pardoned if I say, that his father seemed born to aid in the establishment of our free government, and his mother was a suitable companion and co-laborer of such a patriot. The cradle hymns of the child were the songs of liberty. The power and competence of man for self-government were the topics which he most frequently heard discussed by the wise men of the day, and the inspiration thus caught, gave form and pressure to his after life. Thus early imbued with the love of free institutions, educated by his father for the service of his country, and early led by Washington to its altar, he has stood before the world as one of its eminent statesmen. He has occupied, in turn, almost every place of honor which the country could give him, and for more than half a century has been thus identified with its history. Under any circumstances, I should feel myself unequal to the task of rendering justice to his memory; but, with the debilitating effect of bad health still upon me, I can only with extreme brevity touch upon some of the most prominent features of his life.

While yet a young man, he was, in May, 1794, appointed Minister Resident to the States General of the United Netherlands. In May, 1796, two years after, he was appointed Minister Plenipotentiary at Lisbon, in Portugal. These honors were conferred on him by George Washington, with the advice and consent of the Senate.

In May, 1797, he was appointed Minister Plenipotentiary to the King of Prussia. In March, 1798, and probably while at Berlin, he was appointed a Commissioner, with full powers to negotiate a treaty of amity and commerce with Sweden.

After his return to the United States he was elected by the Legislature of Massachusetts a Senator, and discharged the duties of that station in this chamber from the 4th of March, 1803, until June, 1808, when, differing from his colleague and from the State upon a great political question, he resigned his seat. In June, 1809, he was nominated and appointed Minister Plenipotentiary to the Court of St. Petersburgh.

While at that court, in February, 1811, he was appointed an Associate Justice of the Supreme Court of the United States, to fill a vacancy occasioned by the death of Judge Cushing, but never took his seat upon the bench.

In May, 1813, he, with Messrs. Gallatin and Bayard, was nominated Envoy Extraordinary and Minister Plenipotentiary to negotiate a treaty of peace with Great Britain, under the mediation of Russia, and a treaty of commerce with Russia. From causes which it is unnecessary to notice, nothing was accomplished under this appointment. But afterward, in January, 1814, he, with Messrs. Gallatin, Bayard, Clay, and Russell, were appointed Ministers Plenipotentiary and Extraordinary to negotiate a treaty of peace, and a treaty of commerce with Great Britain. This mission succeeded in effecting a pacification, and the name of Mr. Adams is subscribed to the treaty of Ghent.

After this eventful crisis in our public affairs, he was, in February, 1815, selected by Mr. Madison to represent the country, and protect its interests, at the Court of St. James; and he remained there as Envoy Extraordinary and Minister Plenipotentiary until Mr. Monroe became President of the United States.

On the 5th of March, 1817, at the commencement of the new administration, he was appointed Secretary of State, and continued in the office while that gentleman was at the head of the administration.

In 1825, he was elected his successor, and discharged the duties of President for one term, ending on the third of March, 1829.

Here followed a brief period of repose from public service, and Mr. Adams retired to his family mansion at Quincy; but was elected a member of the House of Representatives, from the district in which he lived, at the next election which occurred after his return to it, and took his seat in December, 1831. He retained it, by successive elections, to the day of his death.

I have not ventured, on this occasion, beyond a bare enumeration of the high places of trust and confidence which have been conferred upon the deceased. The service covers a period of more than half a century; and what language can I employ which will portray more forcibly the great merits of the deceased, the confidence reposed in him by the public, or the ability with which he discharged the duties devolved upon him, than by this simple narration of recorded facts? An ambitious man could not desire a more emphatic eulogy.

Mr. Adams, however, was not merely a statesman, but a ripe, accomplished scholar, who, during a life of remarkably well-directed industry, made those great acquirements which adorned his character, and gave to it the manly strength of wisdom and intelligence.

As a statesman and patriot, he will rank among the illustrious men of an age prolific in great names, and greatly distinguished for its progress in civilization. The productions of his pen are proofs of a vigorous mind, imbued with a profound knowledge of what it investigates, and of a memory which was singularly retentive and capacious.

But his character is not made up of those conspicuous qualities alone. He will be remembered for the virtues of private life for his elevated moral example, for his integrity, for his devotion to his duties as a Christian, as a neighbor, and as the head of a family. In all these relations, few persons have set a more steadfast or brighter example, and few have descended to the grave where the broken ties of social and domestic affection have been more sincerely lamented. Great as may be the loss to the public of one so gifted and wise, it is by the family that his death will be most deeply felt. His aged and beloved partner, who has so long shared the honors of his career, and to whom all who know her are bound by the ties of friendship, will believe that we share her grief, mourn her bereavement, and sympathize with her in her affliction.

It is believed to have been the earnest wish of his heart to die, like Chatham, in the midst of his labors. It was a sublime thought, that where he had toiled in the house of the nation, in hours of the day devoted to its service, the stroke of death should reach him, and there sever the ties of love and patriotism which bound him to earth. He fell in his seat, attacked by paralysis, of which he had before been a subject. To describe the scene which ensued would be impossible. It was more than the spontaneous gush of feeling which all such events call forth, so much to the honor of our nature. It was the expression of reverence for his moral worth, of admiration for his great intellectual endowments, and of veneration for his age and public services. All gathered round the sufferer, and the strong sympathy and deep feeling which were manifested, showed that the business of the House (which was instantly adjourned) was forgotten amid the distressing anxieties of the moment. He was soon removed to the apartment of the Speaker, where he remained, surrounded by afflicted friends, till the weary clay resigned its immortal spirit. "This is the end of earth!" Brief but emphatic words. They were among the last uttered by the dying Christian.

Thus has closed the life of one whose purity, patriotism, talents, and learning, have seldom been seriously questioned. To say that he had faults, would only be declaring that he was human. Let him who is exempt from error, venture to point them out. In this long career of public life, it would be strange if the venerable man had not met with many who have differed from him in sentiment, or who have condemned his acts. If there be such, let the mantle of oblivion be thrown over each unkind thought. Let not the grave of the "old man eloquent" be desecrated by unfriendly remembrances, but let us yield our homage to his many virtues, and let it be our prayer that we may so perform our duties here, that, if summoned in a like sudden and appalling manner, we may not be found unprepared or unable to utter his words, "I am composed."

THE

CHARACTER OF MR. ADAMS.

BY THE HON. T. H. BENTON.

THE voice of his native State has been heard, through one of the Senators of Massachusetts, announcing the death of her aged and most distinguished son. It is not unfitting or unbecoming in me to second the motion which has been made, for extending the last honors of the Senate to him who, forty-five years ago, was a member of this body, who, at the time of his death, was among the oldest members of the House of Representatives, and who, putting the years of his service together, was the oldest of all the members of the American government.

The eulogium of Mr. Adams is made in the facts of his life, which the Senator from Massachusetts has so strikingly stated, that, from early manhood to octogenarian age, he has been constantly and most honorably employed in the public service. For a period of more than fifty years, from the time of his first appointment as minister abroad under Washington, to his last election to the House of Representatives by the people of his native district, he has been constantly retained in the public service; and that, not by the favor of a sovereign, or by hereditary title, but by the elections and appointments of republican government. This fact makes the eulogy of the illustrious deceased. For what, except a union of all the qualities which command the esteem and confidence of man, could have ensured a public service so long, by appointments free and popular, and from sources so various and exalted? Minister many times abroad; member of this body; member of the House of Representatives; cabinet minister; President of the United States; such has been the galaxy of his splendid appointments. And what but moral excellence the most perfect; intellectual ability the most eminent; fidelity the most unwavering; service the most useful; could have commanded such a succession of appointments so exalted, from sources so various and so eminent? Nothing less could have commanded such a series of appointments; and accordingly we see the union of all these great qualities in him who has received them.

In this long career of public service, Mr. Adams was distinguished not only by faithful attention to all the great duties of his stations, but to all their less and minor duties. He was not the Salaminian galley, to be launched only on extraordinary occasions, but he was the ready vessel, always launched when the duties of his station required it, be the occasion great or small. As President, as cabinet minister, as minister abroad, he examined all questions that came before him, and examined all, in all their parts, in all the minutiæ of their detail, as well as in all the vastness of their comprehension. As Senator, and as a member of the House of Representatives, the obscure committee-room was as much the witness of his laborious application to the drudgery of legislation, as the halls of the two Houses were to the ever ready speech, replete with knowledge, which instructed all hearers, enlightened all subjects, and gave dignity and ornament to debate.

In the observance of all the proprieties of life, Mr. Adams was a most noble and impressive example. He cultivated the minor as well as the greater virtues. Wherever his presence could give aid and countenance to what was useful and honorable to man, there he was. In the exercises of the school and of the college—in the meritorious meetings of the agricultural, mechanical, and commercial societies—in attendance upon divine worship—he gave the punctual attendance rarely seen but in those who are free from the weight of public cares.

Punctual to every duty, death found him at the post of duty;

and where else could it have found him, at any stage of his career, for the fifty years of his illustrious public life? From the time of his first appointment by Washington to his last election by the people of his native town, where could death have found him but at the post of duty? At that post, in the fullness of age, in the ripeness of renown, crowned with honors, surrounded by his family, his friends, and admirers, and in the very presence of the national representation, he has been gathered to his fathers, leaving behind him the memory of public services which are the history of his country for half a century, and the example of a life, public and private, which should be the study and the model of the generations of his countrymen.

POEMS.

THE WANTS OF MAN.*

"Man wants but little here below,
Nor wants that little long."—*Goldsmith's Hermit.*

I.

"Man wants but little here below,
Nor wants that little long."
'Tis not with ME exactly so,
But 'tis so in the song.
My wants are many, and if told
Would muster many a score;
And were each wish a mint of gold,
I still should long for more.

* It was written under these circumstances:—General Ogle informed Mr. Adams that several young ladies in his district had requested him to procure Mr. A.'s autograph for them. In accordance with this request, Mr. Adams wrote the following beautiful poem upon "The Wants of Man," each stanza upon a sheet of note paper.

II.

What first I want is daily bread,
  And canvas backs and wine;
And all the realms of nature spread
  Before me when I dine.
Four courses scarcely can provide
  My appetite to quell,
With four choice cooks from France, beside,
  To dress my dinner well.

III.

What next I want, at heavy cost,
  Is elegant attire;—
Black sable furs, for winter's frost,
  And silks for summer's fire,
And Cashmere shawls, and Brussels lace
  My bosom's front to deck,
And diamond rings my hands to grace,
  And rubies for my neck.

IV.

And then I want a mansion fair,
  A dwelling house, in style,
Four stories high, for wholesome air—
  A massive marble pile;
With halls for banquets and balls,
  All furnished rich and fine;
With stabled studs in fifty stalls,
  And cellars for my wine.

V.

I want a garden and a park,
  My dwelling to surround—
A thousand acres (bless the mark),
  With walls encompassed round—
Where flocks may range and herds may low,
  And kids and lambkins play,
And flowers and fruits commingled grow,
  All Eden to display.

VI.

I want, when summer's foliage falls,
  And autumn strips the trees,
A house within the city's walls,
  For comfort and for ease.
But here, as space is somewhat scant,
  And acres somewhat rare,
My house in town I only want
  To occupy——a square.

VII.

I want a steward, butler, cooks;
  A coachman, footman, grooms,
A library of well-bound books,
  And picture-garnished rooms;
Corregios, Magdalen, and Night,
  The matron of the chair;
Guido's fleet coursers in their flight,
  And Claudes at least a pair.

VIII.

I want a cabinet profuse
  Of medals, coins, and gems;
A printing press, for private use,
  Of fifty thousand EMS;
And plants, and minerals, and shells;
  Worms, insects, fishes, birds;
And every beast on earth that dwells,
  In solitude or herds.

IX.

I want a board of burnished plate,
  Of silver and of gold;
Tureens of twenty pounds in weight,
  With sculpture's richest mould;
Plateaus, with chandeliers and lamps,
  Plates, dishes—all the same;
And porcelain vases, with the stamps
  Of Sevres, Angouleme.

X.

And maples, of fair glossy stain,
  Must form my chamber doors,
And carpets of the Wilton grain
  Must cover all my floors;
My walls, with tapestry bedeck'd,
  Must never be outdone;
And damask curtains must protect
  Their colors from the sun.

XI.

And mirrors of the largest pane
  From Venice must be brought;
And sandal-wood, and bamboo cane,
  For chairs and tables bought;
On all the mantel-pieces, clocks
  Of thrice-gilt bronze must stand,
And screens of ebony and box
  Invite the stranger's hand.

XII.

I want (who does not want?) a wife,
  Affectionate and fair,
To solace all the woes of life,
  And all its joys to share;
Of temper sweet, of yielding will,
  Of firm, yet placid mind,
With all my faults to love me still,
  With sentiment refin'd.

XIII.

And as Time's car incessant runs,
  And Fortune fills my store,
I want of daughters and of sons
  From eight to half a score.
I want (alas! can mortal dare
  Such bliss on earth to crave?)
That all the girls be chaste and fair—
  The boys all wise and brave.

XIV.

And when my bosom's darling sings,
  With melody divine,
A pedal harp of many strings
  Must with her voice combine.
A piano, exquisitely wrought,
  Must open stand, apart,
That all my daughters may be taught
  To win the stranger's heart.

XV.

My wife and daughters will desire
  Refreshment from perfumes,
Cosmetics for the skin require,
  And artificial blooms.
The civit fragrance shall dispense,
  And treasur'd sweets return;
Cologne revive the flagging sense,
  And smoking amber burn.

XVI.

And when at night my weary head
  Begins to droop and dose,
A southern chamber holds my bed,
  For nature's soft repose;
With blankets, counterpanes, and sheet,
  Mattrass, and bed of down,
And comfortables for my feet,
  And pillows for my crown.

XVII.

I want a warm and faithful friend,
  To cheer the adverse hour,
Who ne'er to flatter will descend,
  Nor bend the knee to power;
A friend to chide me when I'm wrong,
  My inmost soul to see;
And that my friendship prove as strong
  For him, as his for me.

XVIII.

I want a kind and tender heart,
  For others wants to feel;
A soul secure from Fortune's dart,
  And bosom arm'd with steel;
To bear divine chastisement's rod.
  And mingling in my plan,
Submission to the will of God,
  With charity to man.

XIX.

I want a keen, observing eye,
  An ever-listening ear,
The truth through all disguise to spy,
  And wisdom's voice to hear;
A tongue, to speak at virtue's need,
  In Heaven's sublimest strain;
And lips, the cause of man to plead,
  And never plead in vain.

XX. 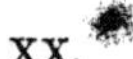

I want uninterrupted health,
  Throughout my long career,
And streams of never-failing wealth,
  To scatter far and near;
The destitute to clothe and feed,
  Free bounty to bestow;
Supply the helpless orphan's need,
  And soothe the widow's woe.

XXI.

I want the genius to conceive,
  The talents to unfold,
Designs, the vicious to retrieve,
  The virtuous to uphold;
Inventive power, combining skill,
  A persevering soul,
Of human hearts to mould the will,
  And reach from pole to pole.

XXII.

I want the seals of power and place,
  The ensigns of command,
Charged by the people's unbought grace,
  To rule my native land.
Nor crown, nor sceptre would I ask
  But from my country's will,
By day, by night, to ply the task
  Her cup of bliss to fill.

XXIII.

I want the voice of honest praise
  To follow me behind,
And to be thought in future days
  The friend of human kind;
That after ages, as they rise,
  Exulting may proclaim,
In choral union to the skies,
  Their blessings on my name

XXIV.

These are the wants of mortal man;
  I cannot want them long,
For life itself is but a span,
  And earthly bliss a song.
My last great want, absorbing all,
  Is, when beneath the sod,
And summon'd to my final call,
  The mercy of my God.

XXV.

And oh! while circles in my veins
  Of life the purple stream,
And yet a fragment small remains
  Of nature's transient dream,
My soul, in humble hope unscar'd,
  Forget not thou to pray,
That this thy WANT may be prepared
  To meet the Judgment Day.

THE PLAGUE IN THE FOREST.

Time was, when round the lion's den,
A peopled city raised its head;
'Twas not inhabited by men,
But by four-footed beasts instead.
The lynx, the leopard, and the bear,
The tiger and the wolf, were there;
The hoof-defended steed;
The bull, prepared with horns to gore,
The cat with claws, the tusky boar,
And all the canine breed.

In social compact thus combined,
Together dwelt the beasts of prey;
Their murderous weapons all resigned,
And vowed each other not to slay.
Among them Reynard thrust his phiz;
Not hoof, nor horn, nor tusk was his,
For warfare all unfit;
He whispered to the royal dunce,
And gained a settlement at once;
His weapon was,—his wit.

One summer, by some fatal spell,
(Phœbus was peevish for some scoff,)
The plague upon that city fell,
And swept the beasts by thousands off.
The lion, as became his part,
Loved his own people from his heart,
And taking counsel sage,
His peerage summoned to advise
And offer up a sacrifice,
To soothe Apollo's rage.

Quoth lion, " We are sinners all,
And even it must be confessed,
If among sheep I chance to fall,—
I, I am guilty as the rest.
To me the sight of lamb is curst,
It kindles in my throat a thirst,—
I struggle to refrain,—
Poor innocent! his blood so sweet!
His flesh so delicate to eat!
I find resistance vain.

" Now to be candid, I must own
The sheep are weak and I am strong,
But when we find ourselves alone,
The sheep have never done me wrong.
And, since I purpose to reveal
All my offences, nor conceal

One trespass from your view ;
My appetite is made so keen,
That with the sheep the time has been
I took,—the shepherd too.

" Then let us all our sins confess,
And whosesoe'er the blackest guilt,
To ease my people's deep distress,
Let *his* atoning blood be spilt.
My own confession now you hear,
Should none of deeper dye appear,
Your sentence freely give ;
And if on me should fall the lot,
Make me the victim on the spot,
And let my people live."

The council with applauses rung,
To hear the Codrus of the wood ;
Though still some doubt suspended hung,
If he would make his promise good,—
Quoth Reynard,—" Since the world was made,
Was ever love like this displayed ?
Let us like subjects true
Swear, as before your feet we fall,
Sooner than you should die for all,
We all will die for you.

" But please your majesty, I deem,
Submissive to your royal grace,

You hold in far too high esteem
   That paltry, poltroon, sheepish race;
For oft, reflecting in the shade,
I ask myself why sheep were made
   By all-creating power?
And howsoe'er I tax my mind,
This the sole reason I can find,
   For lions to devour.

"And as for eating now and then,
   As well the shepherd as the sheep,—
How can that braggart breed of men
   Expect with you the peace to keep?
'Tis time their blustering boast to stem,
That all the world was made for them,
   And prove creation's plan;
Teach them by evidence profuse
That man was made for lion's use,
   Not lions made for man."

And now the noble peers begin,
   And, cheered with such examples bright,
Disclosing each his secret sin,
   Some midnight murder brought to light;
Reynard was counsel for them all,
No crime the assembly could appal,
   But *he* could botch with paint:
Hark! as his honeyed accents roll,
Each tiger is a gentle soul:
   Each blood-hound is a saint.

When each had told his tale in turn,
The long-eared beast of burden came,
And meekly said, "My bowels yearn
To make confession of my shame;
But I remember on a time
I passed, not thinking of a crime,
A haystack on my way:
His lure some tempting devil spread,
I stretched across the fence my head,
And cropped,—a lock of hay."

"Oh, monster! villain!" Reynard cried,—
"No longer seek the victim, sire;
Nor why your subjects thus have died,
To expiate Apollo's ire."
The council with one voice decreed;
All joined to execrate the deed,—
"What, steal another's grass!"
The blackest crime *their* lives could show,
Was washed as white as virgin snow;
The victim was,—The Ass.

TO A BEREAVED MOTHER.

SURE, to the mansions of the blest
  When *infant* innocence ascends,
Some angel, brighter than the rest,
  The spotless spirit's flight attends.
On wings of ecstasy they rise,
  Beyond where worlds material roll;
Till some fair sister of the skies
  Receives the unpolluted soul.

That inextinguishable beam,
  With dust united at our birth,
Sheds a more dim, discolor'd gleam
  The more it lingers upon earth.
Closed in this dark abode of clay,
  The stream of glory faintly burns:—
Not unobserved, the lucid ray
  To its own native fount returns.

But when the LORD of mortal breath
  Decrees his bounty to resume,
And points the silent shaft of death
  Which speeds an infant to the tomb—

No passion fierce, nor low desire,
Has quenched the radiance of the flame;
Back to its God the living fire
Reverts, unclouded as it came.

Fond mourner! be that solace thine!
Let hope her healing charm impart,
And soothe, with melodies divine,
The anguish of a mother's heart.
O, think! the darlings of thy love,
Divested of this earthly clod,
Amid unnumber'd saints above,
Bask in the bosom of their God.

Of their short pilgrimage on earth
Still tender images remain:
Still, still they bless thee for their birth,
Still filial gratitude retain.
Each anxious care, each rending sigh,
That wrung for them the parent's breast,
Dwells on remembrance in the sky,
Amid the raptures of the blest.

O'er thee, with looks of love, they bend;
For thee the Lord of life implore;
And oft, from sainted bliss descend,
Thy wounded quiet to restore.

Oft, in the stillness of the night,
They smooth the pillow of thy bed;
Oft, till the morn's returning light,
Still watchful hover o'er thy head.

Hark! in such strains as saints employ,
They whisper to thy bosom peace;
Calm the perturbed heart to joy,
And bid the streaming sorrow cease.
Then dry, henceforth, the bitter tear:
Their part and thine inverted see:—
Thou wert their guardian angel here,
They guardian angels now to thee.

CHARLES THE FIFTH'S CLOCKS.

WITH Charles the Fifth art thou acquainted, reader?
Of Ferdinand and Isabel the grandson,
In ages past of Europe's realms file leader,
Among the mightiest of all ages, one.
Spain, Germany, his sceptre swayed,
With feet victorious over France he trod,
Afric' and Italy his laws obeyed,
And either India trembled at his nod.
Well, reader, this same monarch mighty,
Like many of his stamp before,
Down to the latest of the set
Whose names I leave in blank, as yet!
And with Napoleon you may fill,
Or Alexander, as you will;
Charles, seated upon all his thrones,
With all his crowns upon his head,
Built piles on piles of human bones,
As if he meant to reign the sovereign of the dead.
He kept the world in uproar forty years,
And waded bloody oceans through;
Feasted on widows' and on orphans' tears,
And cities sacked, and millions slew.

And all the pranks of conquering heroes play'd,
A master workman at the royal trade,
The recipe approved time out of mind,
To win the hearts of all mankind.
But heroes, too, get weary of their trade;
Charles had a conscience, and grew old;
The gout sometimes an ugly visit paid;
A voice within unwelcome stories told,
That heroes, just like common men,
One day must die; and then
Of what might happen Charles was sore afraid.
Of Charles's wars, need little here be said;
Their causes were ambition, avarice, pride,
Despotic empire o'er the world to spread,
Revenge on Francis, who proclaimed *he lied*,
And chiefly Luther's heresies to quell;
To prove the wrong of Reformation
With fire, and sword, and desolation,
And save the souls of Protestants from hell.
But when the humor came to save his own,
Charles stripp'd off all his royal robes,
Dismissed his double globes,
Cast down his crowns, descended from his throne,
And with St. Jerome's monks retired, to die alone.
Charles had a maggot in the mind,
Restless, that needs must be of something thinking;
And now, to keep his spirits from sinking,
Employment often at a loss to find,
Much of his time he spent in prayer;

In penance for his evil deeds,
In saying masses, and in telling beads;
In self-chastisement, till he bled
A drop for every ton of others shed;
And much his little garden claim'd his care,
In planting cabbages and plucking seeds;
But these were simple occupations,
And Charles, so long in empire's toils immers'd,
So deep in all their intricacies vers'd,
Some pastime needed, full of complications.
So long his study had been *man*,
His sport, his victim, *man*, of flesh and blood,
That now with art mechanic he began
To fashion manakins of wood.
Soon he became a skilful mechanician,
And made his mimic men with so much art,
They made St. Jerome's friars start,
And think their royal master a magician,
Leagued with the mother of all evil;
Like Dr. Faustus, soul-bound to the devil.
At last the fancy seized his brain,
Of perfect instruments for keeping time.
Watches and clocks he made, but all in vain;
He never could succeed to make them chime.
With choice chronometers he lin'd his cell;
No two at once would ever ring the bell.
Now mark the moral of my tale,
Which flash'd in sunbeams upon Charles's soul;
When he whose chisel could prevail

Man's outward actions to control,
So that his puppets seemed as good
As living men, though made of wood,
Yet ever baffled found his skill
To mould two watches to his will.
He smote his bosom with a sigh,
Exclaiming, "What a dolt was I,
By force constraining men to think alike,
And cannot make two clocks together strike!"

RETROSPECTION.

WHEN life's fair dream has passed away
  To three score years and ten,
Before we turn again to clay
  The lot of mortal men,
'Tis wise a backward eye to cast
  On life's revolving scene,
With calmness to review the past
  And ask what we have been.

The cradle and the mother's breast
  Have vanish'd from the mind,
Of joys the sweetest and the best,
  Nor left a trace behind.
Maternal tenderness and care
  Were lavished all in vain—
Of bliss; whatever was our share
  No vestiges remain.

Far distant, like a beacon light
  On ocean's boundless waste,
A single spot appears in sight
  Yet indistinctly traced.

Some mimic stage's thrilling cry,
  Some agony of fear,
Some painted wonder to the eye,
  Some trumpet to the ear.

These are the first events of life
  That fasten on the brain,
And through the world's incessant strife
  Indelible remain.
They form the link with ages past
  From former worlds a gleam;
With murky vapors overcast,
  The net-work of a dream.

4

TO THE SUN-DIAL,

UNDER THE WINDOW OF THE HALL OF THE HOUSE OF REPRESENTATIVES OF THE UNITED STATES.

Thou silent herald of Time's silent flight!
Say, could'st thou speak, what warning voice were thine?
Shade, who canst only show how others shine!
Dark, sullen witness of resplendent light
In day's broad glare, and when the moontide bright
Of laughing fortune sheds the ray divine,
Thy ready favors cheer us—but decline
The clouds of morning and the gloom of night.
Yet are thy counsels faithful, just, and wise;
They bid us seize the moments as they pass—
Snatch the retrieveless sunbeam as it flies,
Nor lose one sand of life's revolving glass—
Aspiring still, with energy sublime,
By virtuous deeds to give eternity to Time.

THE THIRTEENTH SATIRE OF JUVENAL.*

FROM Virtue's paths, when hapless men depart,
The first avenger is the culprit's heart;
There sits a judge, from whose severe decree
No strength can rescue, and no speed can flee;
A judge, unbiass'd by the quibbling tribe!
A judge, whom India's treasures cannot bribe.
Calvin, what thinkest thou the world will say,
To see thy faithless friend his trust betray?
Yet, to thy fortune, is the breach but small;
Thy purse will scarcely feel the loss at all;
Nor are examples of such baseness rare!
'Tis what in common with thee thousands bear;
A single drop of water from the deep!
A single grain from fortune's boundless heap.
Excessive sorrow let us then restrain:
A *man* should measure by the wound his pain!

* THE ARGUMENT.—Calvinus had deposited a sum of money in the hands of a friend, who, upon being required to restore it, denied having ever received the trust. Calvinus appears to have been too much affected at this incident, and Juvenal addressed to him this Satire, containing topics of consolation to Calvinus for his loss, and of reproof for the extreme sensibility he had manifested upon the occasion.

Though keen thy sense, the smallest ill to meet,
Must thy blood boil to find thy friend a cheat?
The sacred trust committed he denies—
But, at thy age, can treachery surprise?
When threescore winters thou hast left behind,
To long experience art thou still so blind?
Great, and prevailing is the sacred lore,
Which Wisdom, Fortune's victress, has in store;
But *we* consider likewise those as blest,
Who meet the woes of life with placid breast;
Bred in life's school, who bend beneath her sway,
Nor from her yoke would draw their necks away.
Is there a day so festive through the year,
But frequent frauds and perfidies appear?
A single day, but sees triumphant vice
With lurking dagger, or with loaded dice?
Small is the train who honor's path pursue;
The friends of virtue are a chosen few—
So few, that gathering o'er the spacious earth
A full collection of untainted worth,
Scarce could you find a number, free from guile,
To match the gates of Thebes, or mouths of Nile.
Such are the horrors of our modern times,
They bleach the blackness of all former crimes.
The age of iron has long since been past,
And four besides, each blacker than the last;
A ninth succeeds, compared with which, of old,
The age of iron was an age of gold;
An age, which nature dares not even name,

Nor yields a metal to express its shame.
The faith of gods and men our lips attest,
Loud as a great man's pimps applaud his jest.
But hoary infant; art thou still to know
With what bright charms another's treasures glow?
Go! fetch the rattle of thy childhood, go!
What peals of laughter rise on every side!
How all the town thy simpleness deride!
To see thee ask, and with a serious brow,
That any mortal be not perjured now;
To see thee now, of any man require
Faith in a god, and terror of hell-fire.
These tenets truly our forefathers held,
Ere from this throne old Saturn was expelled,
Before he laid his diadem aside,
And in the rustic sickle took a pride,
While Ida's caves were yet the haunts of Jove,
Nor virgin Juno, conscious of his love.
No revels then were ever seen to rise
Among the heavenly tenants of the skies;
No Trojan boy, no Hebe's form divine,
To fill the goblets with inflaming wine;
With unwashed hands, no smutty Vulcan came
To quaff the nectar, from his anvil's flame.
Each god was then content to dine alone,
Nor was our motley mob of god-heads known;
Small were the numbers of the blest abode;
Nor weighed down wretched Atlas with the load;
No gloomy Pluto ruled the realms of shade,

Nor yet had ravished the Sicilian maid.
Hell then no wheel, no rock, no furies bore,
No vulture's pounces dripped with ghostly gore;
But cheerful spirits ranged the valleys gay,
Nor of infernal monarchs owned the sway.
A fraud was held a wonder in that age;
And in the presence of a hoary sage,
Had any younger man to rise forborne,
However blest with ampler stores of corn,
To them a crime of dye so black it seemed,
As by naught else but death could be redeemed.
The like respect by beardless boys was shown
To those whose faces were but just o'ergrown;
Such awe four years precedence could engage,
And youth's first blossom bore the fruits of age!
Now, if your friend should not betray his trust,
But give you back your coins with all their rust,
It seems a miracle of higher strain,
Than all the Tuscan sybil books contain,
And, in memorial of so strange a deed,
A votive lamb should on the altar bleed.
If now mine eyes a man of virtue greet,
I think a double-headed child to meet
Not more surprising were it to behold
A plough-share dig up fish, or mules with foal;
Rain fall in pebbles, or in wildest shapes
Bees, clustering on a temple's roof like grapes,
Or rivers, rushing with tremendous sweep,
To pour a milky torrent in the deep.

The loss of fifty ducats you deplore,
See your next neighbor filched of ten times more;
By a like fraud behold a third complain
His loss of all his strong-box could contain.
So prone, so ready are we to despise
The single testimonial of the skies,
Unless a mortal sanction too be given,
And *man* confirm the evidence of *Heaven!*
Look! with what seeming purity of breast
And steady face he dares his faith attest
Swears by the solar beams, the bolts of Jove,
And thy full quiver, huntress of the grove;
By Mars' lance, Apollo's arrows drear,
By Neptune's trident, and Minerva's spear,
Alcides' bow, and whatsoe'er beside
From all heaven's arsenal can be supplied;
And, if a father—sooner be my food
My infant's flesh, he cries, my drink his blood!
There are who deem that Fortune governs all;
That no Supreme Disposer rules the ball;
That Nature's energies alone suffice
To make successive days and seasons rise;
Hence, with intrepid brow, such men as these
To sanction falsehood, any altar seize,
Another trembles lest the vengeance due,
Of gods offended, should his crimes pursue;
Believes in gods, yet stains with guilt his soul,
Aud thus attempts his terrors to control
"Deal with my body as thou wilt," he cries,

"Great Isis! and with blindness strike my eyes,
If peacefully, though blind, I may but hold
The price of perjury, the pilfered gold.
What is a palsied side, a broken leg,
Compared with indigence, compelled to beg
The fleetest runner would, beyond a doubt,
Give all his swiftness for a wealthy gout;
Nay, should he hesitate in such a case,
Send for his doctor and his waistcoat lace;
For what can all his racing talent boot?
A hungry stomach and a nimble foot.
And what avails the olive round his head,
While puffed with glory, he must pine for bread?
The anger of the gods, though great, is slow;
Nor will their mercy doom to endless woe;
And if they punish every guilty soul,
Before my turn comes what long years may roll!
Perhaps their wrath is pacified with ease,
And oft they overlook such faults as these;
For the same deed, as good or ill luck reigns,
One wields a sceptre, and one hangs in chains."
  Thus having lulled his conscience to repose,
Before you to the sacred fane he goes;
Nay, drags you thither, with indignant ear
The oath of fraud and perfidy to hear;
For, with the multitude, guilt's face of brass
For conscious innocence will often pass.
See! how he lays his hand upon his heart,
And like a finished actor plays his part!

You, plunder'd of your trust, with piercing cries,
In vain, with voice like Stentor, rend the skies,
Or rather, like old Homer's Mars exclaim,
"Hear'st thou all this, great Jove, in silence tame,
When all thy fury, at such vows accurst,
From lips of brass or marble ought to burst?
Else, wherefore burns our incense at thy shrine?
Why, on thy altars, bleed the calves or swine?
Since no distinction, I perceive, were just,
Between your statues and a dancer's bust."
Yet hear what comfort an unlettered friend,
Though from no school derived, can recommend;
Who never made the cynic rule his own,
Nor that of stoics, differing but in gown;
Nor yet has learned the maxims to obey
Of Epicurus, in his garden gay.
When dire diseases rack your feeble frame,
Call for some doctor of distinguished fame;
But in a case like yours, of trifling pain,
To Philip's pupil you may trust your vein.
Expressly show that since the world began
A deed so base was never done by man;
Then, I object no longer, tear your hair,
And beat your face and bosom in despair;
At such a dread misfortune close your gates,
With lamentation loud accuse the Fates,
Heave deeper groans, tears more abundant shed
For money pilfered than a father dead.
No man in this case feigns of grief a show;

Content to wear the formal suits of woe,
And fret his eyes to strain a seeming tear,
No! for lost gold our sorrows are sincere!
But if the like complaint with yours you meet,
Where'er you turn your eyes in every street;
If every day shows men who boldly dare
Their own hand-writing to a bond forswear;
Proved by ten witnesses their deed deny,
And gravely give their solemn seal the lie,
Must thou from common miseries be free?
And art thou formed of better clay than we?
Thou, favored by the gods with special grace;
We, the vile refuse of a worthless race?
Thine eyes to crimes of deeper baseness turn,
And thy small loss to bear with patience learn;
See this man's slave with robber bands conspire,
Behold that mansion blaze with bidden fire:
See, from yon antique temple stolen away,
The massive goblet, venerably gray!
Gifts from which nations once derived renown,
Or some old monarch's consecrated crown.
Are these not there? behold the villain ply
To rasp the gilding from Alcides' thigh,
Strike off the nose from Neptune's aged form,
Or strip the bracelet from young Castor's arm;
Why should he dread of minor gods the frown,
Wont the whole thunderer bravely to melt down?
The guilt of blood see other wretches share,
And one the poison sell, and one prepare!

See, to a harmless, hapless, monkey tied,
Plunged in the briny deep the parricide;
Yet in this list how small a part appear
Of all the crimes that meet the Prætor's ear,
And he from Hesper's dawn till closing day must hear.
The manners of mankind wouldst thou be taught,
With full instruction that one house is fraught;
But a few days attend the trials there,
And then to call thyself unhappy, dare.
Who feels astonishment affect his mind
Amidst the Alps a tumid throat to find?
Or who behold in Meroe, with surprise,
A dug surpass the child it feeds in size?
On seeing Germans, who would think to stare
At azure eyes and golden-colored hair,
And crisped locks, with ointments which distill?
Such they were made by Nature's sovereign will
Clap but a cloud of Thracian cranes their wings,
Lo! to his arms the pigmy warrior springs!
But soon, unequal to resistance, flies,
Clenched in relentless clutches through the skies.
Among ourselves a sight like this would make
Your sides, no doubt, with ceaseless laughter shake;
But there, though common, 'tis no laughing sight,
Where the whole tribe is not a foot in height.
"But shall the wretch all penalties evade,
For friendship perjur'd, and for trust betrayed?"
Suppose him seized, in chains, and at your will,
(What would vindictive anger more?) to kill;

Yet would your damage still the same remain,
Nor could his death restore the trust again;
How poor a comfort, to relieve your woe,
The blood that from his headless trunk would flow!
"But vengeance, even more than life, is sweet;"
Yes! to those minds of heedless, headlong heat,
Which blaze at every spark, however small,
And often kindle without cause at all:
Not Thales thus, nor thus Chrysippus speaks,
Not thus the best and wisest of the Greeks—
The godlike Socrates—who, galled with chains,
To share the hemlock with his foe disdains.
True wisdom points to virtue's path, and frees
From every vice and error, by degrees;
The noble soul above revenge we find,
'Tis the poor pleasure of a puny mind:
If proof you need, contemplate female spite;
In vengeance none like women take delight.
But, canst thou deem from all chastisement freed
Men who beneath the scourge of conscience bleed?
By scorpions stung, their teeth in fury gnash,
And writhe with anguish at the secret lash?
Oh! trust me, friend, the judge in hell below
Cannot on crimes inflict so deep a woe
As that poor mortal feels, by guilt oppressed,
Doomed day and night to bear the witness in his breast.
A Spartan once to Delphi's fane repaired,
And to consult the god's opinion dared,
Whether he might retain entrusted gold,

And with a solemn oath the fraud uphold!
The priestess answered, with indignant air,
The doubt alone its punishment should bear;
Th' insulting doubt that in the question lies,
If great Apollo would a crime advise.
The frightened Spartan, by compulsion just,
From fear, not virtue, straight restored the trust;
Yet soon he found, that, from the sacred fane,
His doom deserved was not denounced in vain:
Himself, his offspring, all his hapless race,
Swept from the earth, left not behind a trace.
By such hard penalties must men atone
The fault of meditated wrong alone;
He guilt incurs who merely guilt intends—
How much more he, then, who in act offends?
Perpetual anguish preys upon his breast,
Nor, even at his meals, allows him rest.
His sickened palate, nauseating, heaves
At every morsel that his mouth receives;
Loathes the fine fragrance of long-hoarded vines,
The cordial drop, distilled from Alban wines;
While his knit brows, if choicer still you bring,
Of sour Falernian seem to mark the sting.
At night, if when his limbs have long been spread,
In restless tossings, over all his bed,
Short slumber comes at last to close his eyes,
In dreams he sees the hallowed temple rise
Before him violated altars stand,
And gods offended, with uplifted hand;

But, what his breast with torture chiefly rends
Larger than life thy sacred form ascends,
With deadly fears his dastard soul to press,
And force his lips their falsehood to confess.
Heaven's earliest murmurs cause his heart to fail,
And every flash of lightning turns him pale;
By storms or chance impelled, no bolts can fly,
He thinks, but vengeance hurls it from on high.
If, yet unhurt, he sees one storm pass o'er.
He only trembles at the next the more.
If in his side he feels the slightest pains,
Or sleepless fever riot in his veins,
The weapons of a god he fancies these,
Sent to afflict his body with disease.
For health he dares not ask the powers divine,
With votive offerings at the sacred shrine;
For oh! what mercy can the guilty mind,
In illness, hope from angry heaven to find?
What bleeding victims for his crimes atone,
Whose life were not more precious than his own?
With what a changeful, sickliness of soul,
The varying tempers of the wicked roll!
Crimes to commit how bold they are and strong!
But soon they learn to know the right from wrong.
Yet stubborn nature all amendment spurns,
And to her evil practices returns.
For what offender ever yet was found
Who to his vices could prescribe a bound?
The blush of shame, when once expelled the face,

Who ever saw it reassume its place?
In all thy life's experience, hast thou known
A man contented with one crime alone?

The wretch who wronged you, in the toils soon caught,
Shall to some prison's gloomy cell be brought;
Or to some dreary rock of banishment,
For famous exiles noted, shall be sent;
Then shall the sufferings of your perjured foe
Sweet consolation on your soul bestow;
And then, at last, shall your rejoicing mind
Confess the gods are neither deaf nor blind.

VERSION OF THE ONE HUNDRED SEVENTH PSALM.

O THAT the race of men would raise
  Their voices to their heavenly King,
And with the sacrifice of praise
  The glories of Jehovah sing!—
Ye navigators of the sea,
  Your course on ocean's tides who keep,
And there Jehovah's wonders see,
  His wonders in the briny deep!

He speaks; conflicting whirlwinds fly;
  The waves in swelling torrents flow;
They mount, aspire to heaven on high;
  They sink, as if to hell below:
Their souls with terror melt away;
  They stagger as if drunk with wine
Their skill is vain,—to thee they pray;
  O, save them, Energy divine!

He stays the storm; the waves subside;
  Their hearts with rapture are inspired;
Soft breezes waft them o'er the tide,
  In gladness, to their port desired:

O that mankind the song would raise,
  Jehovah's goodness to proclaim!
Assembled nations shout his praise,
  Assembled elders bless his name!

THE HOUR-GLASS.

Alas! how swift the moments fly!
  How flash the years along!
Scarce here, yet gone already by,
  The burden of a song.
See childhood, youth, and manhood pass,
  And age, with furrowed brow;
Time was—Time shall be—drain the glass—
  But where in Time is *now?*

Time is the measure but of change;
  No present hour is found;
The past, the future, fill the range
  Of Time's unceasing round.
Where, then, is *now?* In realms above,
  With God's atoning Lamb,
In regions of eternal love,
  Where sits enthroned I AM.

Then, pilgrim, let thy joys and tears
  On Time no longer lean;
But henceforth all thy hopes and fears
  From earth's affections wean:

To God let votive accents rise;
With truth, with virtue, live;
So all the bliss that Time denies
Eternity shall give.

SABBATH MORNING.

55

HARK! 'tis the holy temple's bell;
  The voice that summons me to prayer:
My heart, each roving fancy quell;
  Come, to the house of God repair.

44

There, while, in orison sublime,
  Souls to the throne of God ascend,
Let no unhallowed child of time
  Profane pollutions with them blend.

44

How for thy wants canst thou implore,
  Crave for thy frailties pardon free,
Of praise the votive tribute pour,
  Or bend, in thanks, the grateful knee,—

66

If, from the awful King of kings,
  Each bauble lures thy soul astray;
If to this dust of earth it clings,
  And, fickle, flies from heaven away;

Pure as the blessed seraph's vow,
  O, let the sacred concert rise;
Intent with humble rapture bow,
  Adore the ruler of the skies.

Bid earth-born atoms all depart;
  Within thyself collected, fall;
And give one day, rebellious heart,
  Unsullied to the Lord of all

THE DEATH OF CHILDREN.

SURE, to the mansions of the blest
  When infant innocence ascends,
Some angel brighter than the rest
  The spotless spirit's flight attends.

On wings of ecstasy they rise,
  Beyond where worlds material roll
Till some fair sister of the skies
  Receives the unpolluted soul

There, at the Almighty Father's hand,
  Nearest the throne of living light,
The choirs of infant seraphs stand,
  And dazzling shine, where all are bright.

That inextinguishable beam,
  With dust united at our birth,
Sheds a more dim, discolored gleam,
  The more it lingers upon earth.

Closed in this dark abode of clay,
The stream of glory faintly burns,
Nor unobscured the lucid ray
To its own native fount returns.

But when the Lord of mortal breath
Decrees his bounty to resume.
And points the silent shaft of death,
Which speeds an infant to the tomb—

No passion fierce, no low desire,
Has quenched the radiance of the flame;
Back to its God the living fire
Returns, unsullied, as it came

WRITTEN IN SICKNESS.

LORD of all worlds, let thanks and praise
  To thee forever fill my soul;
With blessings thou hast crowned my days—
  My heart, my head, my hand control:
O, let no vain presumption rise,
  No impious murmur in my heart,
To crave the boon thy will denies,
  Or shrink from ill thy hands impart.

Thy child am I, and not an hour,
  Revolving in the orbs above,
But brings some token of thy power,
  But brings some token of thy love:
And shall this bosom dare repine,
  In darkness dare deny the dawn,
Or spurn the treasures of the mine,
  Because one diamond is withdrawn?

The fool denies, the fool alone,
  Thy being, Lord, and boundless might,
Denies the firmament, thy throne,
  Denies the sun's meridian light;

Denies the fashion of his frame,
  The voice he hears, the breath he draws;
O idiot atheist! to proclaim
  Effects unnumbered without cause.

Matter and mind, mysterious one,
  Are man's for threescore years and ten;
Where, ere the thread of life was spun?
  Where, when reduced to dust again?
All-seeing God, the doubt suppress;
  The doubt thou only canst relieve;
My soul thy Saviour-Son shall bless,
  Fly to thy gospel, and believe.

HYMN FOR THE TWENTY-SECOND OF DECEMBER.

When o'er the billow-heaving deep,
  The fathers of our race,
The precepts of their God to keep,
  Sought here their resting-place—

That gracious God their path prepared,
  Preserved from every harm,
And still for their protection bared
  His everlasting arm.

His breath, inspiring every gale,
  Impels them o'er the main;
His guardian angels spread the sail,
  And tempests howl in vain.

For them old ocean's rocks are smoothed;
  December's face grows mild;
To vernal airs her blasts are soothed,
  And all their rage beguiled.

When Famine rolls her haggard eyes,
His ever-bounteous hand
Abundance from the sea supplies,
And treasures from the sand.

Nor yet his tender mercies cease;
His overruling plan
Inclines to gentleness and peace
The heart of savage man.

And can our stony bosoms be
To all these wonders blind?
Nor swell with thankfulness to thee,
O Parent of mankind?

All-gracious God, inflame our zeal;
Dispense one blessing more;
Grant us thy boundless love to feel,
Thy goodness to adore.

O GOD, WITH GOODNESS ALL THY OWN.

O God, with goodness all thy own,
In mercy cause thy face to shine;
So shall thy ways on earth be known,
Thy saving health and power divine:
O, let the gladdening nations sing,
And praise thy name with hallowed mirth,
For thou of righteousness art King,
And rulest all the subject earth.

O, let the people praise the Lord;
The people all thy praise express;
And earth her plenty shall afford,
And God, yea, our own God, shall bless;
Our God his blessing shall bestow;
His power, his goodness, shall appear;
And all the ends of earth shall know
And worship him with holy fear.

SING TO JEHOVAH A NEW SONG.

Sing to Jehovah a new song,
For deeds of wonder he hath done;
His arm in holiness is strong;
His hand the victory hath won:
The Lord salvation hath made known;
His goodness o'er the world extends;
His truth to Israel's house is shown;
His power to earth's remotest ends.

Shout to Jehovah, all the earth,
Break forth in joy, exult, and sing;
Let voice, let clarion speak your mirth,
Trumpet and harp proclaim your King:
Roar, ocean, to thy lowest deep;
Shout, earth, and all therein that dwell;
Floods, clap your hands as on you sweep:
Mountains, the choral anthem swell.

Let heaven, and earth, and sea, combine,
Jehovah's holy name to bless;
Creation owns his power divine,
The universe his righteousness;

He comes in judgment to display
  Resistless right and boundless grace;
The world with equity to sway,
  And blessings shed o'er all our race.

O, ALL YE PEOPLE, CLAP YOUR HANDS.

O, ALL ye people, clap your hands,
Shout unto God with holy mirth;
In fearful majesty he stands;
He is the Monarch of the earth:
Before us nations he subdues,
And prostrates kingdoms at our feet;
For us a portion he shall choose
In favored Jacob's chosen seat.

God, with a shout, to heaven ascends;
Sing praises to our God and King:
Hark! the loud tempest ether rends;
Sing praises, praises, praises sing.
His power Creation's orb sustains;
Sing hymns of praise to him alone:
Jehovah o'er the nations reigns;
He sits upon his holy throne.

See gathering princes, men of might,
In crowds from earth's remotest shore,
With us in worship all unite,
And Abraham's God with us adore:

The shields of earth are all his own,
  And, far o'er human ken sublime,
Eternal pillars prop his throne,
  Beyond the bounds of space and time.

TURN TO THE STARS OF HEAVEN THINE EYES.

Turn to the stars of heaven thine eyes,
  And God shall meet thee there;
Exalt thy vision to the skies,
  His glory they declare;
Day speaks to day, night teaches night,
  The wonders of their frame,
And all in harmony unite
  Their Maker to proclain.

Earth has no language, man no speech,
  But gives their voice a tongue;
Their words the world's foundations reach;
  Their hymn in heaven is sung;
Pavilioned there in glory bright,
  As from a blooming bride,
The sun comes forth in floods of light,
  With all a bridegroom's pride.

Glad, like a giant for the race,
  His orient flame ascends,
Soars through the boundless realms of space,
  And in the west descends;

His heat the vital lamp bestows,
  The firmament pervades,
In ocean's darkest caverns glows,
  And earth's profoundest shades.

O LORD MY GOD! HOW GREAT ART THOU!

55

O Lord my God! how great art thou!
With honor and with glory crowned;
Light's dazzling splendors veil thy brow,
And gird the universe around.

66

Spirits and angels thou hast made;
Thy ministers a flaming fire;
By thee were earth's foundations laid;
At thy rebuke the floods retire.

44

Thine are the fountains of the deep;
By thee their waters swell or fail;
Up to the mountain's summit creep,
Or shrink beneath the lowly vale.

44

Thy fingers mark their utmost bound;
That bound the waters may not pass;
Their moisture swells the teeming ground,
And paints the valleys o'er with grass.

The waving harvest, Lord, is thine;
  The vineyard, and the olive's juice;
Corn, wine, and oil, by thee combine,
  Life, gladness, beauty, to produce.

The moon for seasons thou hast made,
  The sun for change of day and night;
Of darkness thine the deepest shade,
  And thine the day's meridian light.

O Lord, thy works are all divine;
  In wisdom hast thou made them all;
Earth's teeming multitudes are thine;
  Thine—peopled ocean's great and small.

All these on thee for life depend;
  Thy spirit speaks, and they are born;
They gather what thy bounties send;
  Thy hand of plenty fills the horn.

Thy face is hidden—they turn pale,
  With terror quake, with anguish burn;
Their breath thou givest to the gale;
  They die, and to their dust return.

And thou, my soul, with pure delight,
  Thy voice to bless thy Maker raise;
His praise let morning sing to night,
  And night to morn repeat his praise.

O LORD, THY ALL-DISCERNING EYES.

O Lord, thy all-discerning eyes
  My inmost purpose see;
My deeds, my words, my thoughts, arise
  Alike disclosed to thee:
My sitting down, my rising up,
  Broad noon, and deepest night,
My path, my pillow, and my cup,
  Are open to thy sight.

Before, behind, I meet thine eye,
  And feel thy heavy hand:
Such knowledge is for me too high,
  To reach or understand:
What of thy wonders can I know?
  What of thy purpose see?
Where from thy spirit shall I go?
  Where from thy presence flee?

If I ascend to heaven on high,
  Or make my bed in hell;
Or take the morning's wings, and fly
  O'er ocean's bounds to dwell;

Or seek, from thee, a hiding-place
  Amid the gloom of night—
Alike to thee are time and space,
  The darkness and the light.

MY SOUL, BEFORE THY MAKER KNEEL.

My soul, before thy Maker kneel;
His name let all within me bless;
'Tis he the wounded heart shall heal;
'Tis he shall comfort in distress:
My soul, his name forget not thou,
Who e'en in tender mercy frowns,
Forgives thy oft-forgotten vow,
And still thy lips with blessing crowns.

The Lord of mercy and of grace,
To kindness swift, to anger slow,
Not always wears a chiding face,
Not always bends the avenging bow:
Above the earth as heaven is high,
Above our crimes his mercies rise:
We sin—but pardon still is nigh;
Fools—he rewards us as the wise.

Far distant as the adverse poles,
Our sins he scatters to the wild,
Pities the frailties of our souls—
A father's pity for his child:

He knows our frame ;—our days are grass;
  The fading floweret's bloom is o'er;
Let but a breeze of morning pass,
  The place shall never know it more.

But far beyond the bounds of time
  The mercies of the Lord are sure;
Throughout eternity sublime
  His truth and justice shall endure:
His grace of those who keep his law
  Shall on the children's children fall;
His throne high heaven beholds with awe;
  His kingdom ruleth over all.

FOR THEE IN ZION WAITETH PRAISE.

For thee in Zion waiteth praise,
  O God, O thou that hearest prayer;
To thee the suppliant voice we raise;
  To thee shall all mankind repair.
On thee the ends of earth rely;
  In thee the distant seas confide;
By thee the mountains brave the sky,
  And girded by thy strength abide.

Thou speakest to the tempest peace;
  The roaring wave obeys thy nod;
The tumults of the people cease;
  Earth trembles at the voice of God:
The morning's dawn, the evening's shade,
  Alike thy power with gladness see;
The fields from thee the rains receive,
  And swell with fruitfulness by thee.

Thy river, gracious God, o'erflows;
  Its streams for human wants provide;
At thy command the harvest grows,
  By thy refreshing showers supplied:

Thy bounty clothes the plains with grass;
Thy path drops fatness as it goes;
And wheresoe'er thy footsteps pass,
The desert blossoms like the rose.

Thy goodness crowns the circling year;
The wilderness repeats thy voice;
The mountains clad with flocks appear;
The hills on every side rejoice;
And harvests from the valleys spring;
The reaper's sickle they employ;
And, hark! how hill and valley ring
With universal shouts of joy!

MY SHEPHERD IS THE LORD ON HIGH.

My Shepherd is the Lord on high;
His hand supplies me still;
In pastures green he makes me lie,
Beside the rippling rill:
He cheers my soul, relieves my woes,
His glory to display;
The paths of righteousness he shows,
And leads me in his way.

Though walking through death's dismal shade,
No evil will I fear;
Thy rod, thy staff shall lend me aid,
For thou art ever near:
For me a table thou dost spread
In presence of my foes;
With oil thou dost anoint my head;
By thee my cup o'erflows.

Thy goodness and thy mercy sure
Shall bless me all my days;
And I, with lips sincere and pure,
Will celebrate thy praise.

Yes, in the temple of the Lord
Forever I will dwell;
To after time thy name record,
And of thy glory tell.

SEND FORTH, O GOD, THY TRUTH AND LIGHT.

Send forth, O God, thy truth and light,
And let them lead me still,
Undaunted, in the paths of right,
Up to thy holy hill:
Then to thy altar will I spring,
And in my God rejoice
And praise shall tune the trembling string,
And gratitude my voice.

O why, my soul, art thou cast down?
Within me why distressed?
Thy hopes the God of grace shall crown;
He yet shall make thee blessed;
To him, my never-failing Friend,
I bow, and kiss the rod;
To him shall thanks and praise ascend,
My Saviour and my God.

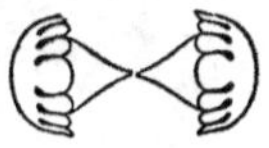

O JUDGE ME, LORD, FOR THOU ART JUST.

O JUDGE me, Lord, for thou art just;
Thy statutes are my pride;
In thee alone I put my trust;
I therefore shall not slide:
O prove me, try my reins and heart;
Thy mercies, Lord, I know;
I never took the scorner's part,
Nor with the vain will go.

Of sinners I detest the bands,
Nor with them will offend;
In innocence will wash my hands,
And at thine altar bend;
There, with thanksgiving's grateful voice,
Thy wondrous works will tell;
I love the mansions of thy choice,
And where thine honors dwell.

O HEAL ME, LORD, FOR I AM WEAK.

O HEAL me, Lord, for I am weak;
My bones are vexed with pain;
Let not thy hot displeasure speak;
Thy burning wrath restrain.
My soul what sore vexations try!
How long shall they assail?
Return, and listen to my cry;
Let mercy, Lord, prevail.

Of thee no memory remains
In death's relentless cave;
To thee ascend no grateful strains
Of glory from the grave:
With ceaseless pain I groan and weep,
So cruel are my foes;
My very couch in tears I steep,
My bed with grief o'erflows.

Depart from me, all who rejoice
Iniquity to share;
The Lord hath heard my moaning voice,
And listened to my prayer;

What though my foes despise the Lord,
   And my destruction plot?
Vexation shall be their reward,
   And sudden shame their lot.

BLEST IS THE MORTAL WHOSE DELIGHT.

Blest is the mortal whose delight
  Is in the precepts of the Lord,
Who meditates them day and night,
  And hears the holy gospel's word;
From the blasphemer's counsel turns,
  Disdains his slanders to repeat,
The luring path of sinners spurns,
  Nor sits upon the scorner's seat.

For him prosperity shall flow;
  Whate'er he undertakes shall thrive;
But with the wicked 'tis not so;
  Like chaff before the wind they drive:
He, like the fruit-tree's planted stem,
  Beside the river's brink shall bear,
While the green leaf shall fade for them,
  Nor wealth nor honors shall they share.

In vain to mortal eyes concealed
  The paths of righteousness and crime
To Heaven's all-seeing eye revealed,
  Man shall discern them, too, in time:

The blessing of the Lord shall fall
  Upon the dwelling of the just;
While, by the doom of sinners, all
  Their hopes shall crumble into dust.

WHY SHOULD I FEAR IN EVIL DAYS.

WHY should I fear in evil days,
  With snares encompassed all around?
What trust can transient treasures raise
  For them in riches who abound?
His brother who from death can save?
  What wealth can ransom him from God?
What mine of gold defraud the grave?
  What hoards but vanish at his nod?

To live forever is their dream;
  Their houses by their name they call;
While, borne by time's relentless stream,
  Around them wise and foolish fall;
Their riches others must divide;
  They plant, but others reap the fruit;
In honor man cannot abide,
  To death devoted, like the brute.

This is their folly, this their way;
  And yet in this their sons delight;
Like sheep, of death the destined prey,
  The future scorn of the upright;

The grave their beauty shall consume,
Their dwellings never see them more;
But God shall raise me from the tomb,
And life for endless time restore.

What though thy foe in wealth increase,
And fame and glory crown his head?
Fear not, for all at death shall cease,
Nor fame, nor glory, crown the dead:
While prospering all around thee smiled,
Yet to the grave shalt thou descend;
The senseless pride of fortune's child
Shall share the brute creation's end.

COME, LET US SING UNTO THE LORD.

Come, let us sing unto the Lord,
  The Rock of our salvation sing,
With joyful noise his praise record,
  And thanks before his presence bring:
Great is Jehovah, great our God,
  Exalted above all his throne;
The depths of earth obey his nod;
  The mountain tops are all his own.

He made the sea; the land he made;
  And both his matchless power reveal:
O, be the Lord our God obeyed;
  O, come, before him let us kneel:
He is our Maker—we his flock,
  His people, by his pastures fed:
Let not your hearts be turned to rock;
  O, hear his warning voice with dread.

SING TO THE LORD A SONG OF PRAISE.

Sing to the Lord a song of praise;
  Assemble, ye who love his name;
Let congregated millions raise
  Triumphant glory's loud acclaim:
From earth's remotest regions come;
  Come, greet your Maker, and your King;
With harp, with timbrel, and with drum,
  His praise let hill and valley sing.

Your praise the Lord will not disdain;
  The humble soul is his delight;
Saints, on your couches swell the strain,
  Break the dull stillness of the night;
Rejoice in glory; bid the storm,
  Bid thunder's voice his praise expand;
And, while your lips the chorus form,
  Grasp for the fight his vengeful brand.

Go forth in arms; Jehovah reigns;
  Their graves let foul oppressors find;
Bind all their sceptred kings in chains;
  Their peers with iron fetters bind.

Then to the Lord shall praise ascend;
  Then all mankind, with one accord,
And freedom's voice, till time shall end,
  In pealing anthems, praise the Lord.

LORD OF ALL WORLDS.

LORD of all worlds, let thanks and praise
 To thee forever fill my soul;
With blessings thou hast crowned my days,—
 My heart, my head, my hand control:
O, let no vain presumptions rise,
 No impious murmur in my heart,
To crave the boon thy will denies,
 Or shrink from ill thy hands impart.

Thy child am I, and not an hour,
 Revolving in the orbs above,
But brings some token of thy power,
 But brings some token of thy love;
And shall this bosom dare repine,
 In darkness dare deny the dawn,
Or spurn the treasures of the mine,
 Because one diamond is withdrawn?

The fool denies, the fool alone,
 Thy being, Lord, and boundless might;
Denies the firmament, thy throne,
 Denies the sun's meridian light;

Denies the fashion of his frame,
  The voice he hears, the breath he draws;
O idiot atheist! to proclaim
  Effects unnumbered without cause!

Matter and mind, mysterious one,
  Are man's for threescore years and ten;
Where, ere the thread of life was spun?
  Where, when reduced to dust again?
All-seeing God, the doubt suppress;
  The doubt thou only canst relieve;
My soul thy Saviour-Son shall bless,
  Fly to thy gospel, and believe.

JUSTICE.

AN ODE.

I.

CHILD of the dust! to yonder skies
  Thy vision canst thou turn?
And trace with perishable eyes,
  The seats where seraphs burn?
There, by the throne of God on high,
An angel form canst thou descry,
  Ineffably sublime?
Or is the effulgence of the Light,
Intense, insufferably bright,
  For beings born of Time?

II.

That angel form, in light enshrined,
  Beside the living throne,
Is Justice, still to heaven confined—
  For God is just alone.
This Angel, of celestial birth,
Her faint resemblance here on earth

Has sent, mankind to guide—
Yet, though obscured her brightest beams,
Still with too vivid ray she gleams
For Mortals to abide.

III.

When the first father of our race
Against his God rebelled,
Was banished from his Maker's face,
From Paradise expelled;
For guilt unbounded to atone,
What bound could punishment have known,
Had Justice dealt the blow?
Sure, to infernal regions hurled,
His doom had been a flaming world
Of never ending woe!

IV.

But Mercy, from the throne of God,
Extended forth her hand;
Withheld th' exterminating rod,
And quenched the flaming brand:
His blood the blest Redeemer gave,
Th' apostate victim's blood to save,
And fill redemption's plan:
Angels proclaimed in choral songs,
"Justice to God alone belongs,
And Mercy pardons man."

V.

When, issuing from the savage wild,
  Man forms the social tie,
Justice severe, and Mercy mild,
  To bind the compact vie;
Of each his own, the parting hedge
Stern Justice takes the solemn pledge;
  The sacred vow enjoins.
While Mercy, with benignant face,
Bids man his fellow-man embrace,
  And heart with heart entwines.

VI.

To both united is the trust
  Of human laws consigned;
One teaches mortals to be just;
  The other, to be kind;
Yet shall not Justice always wear
The garb of punishment, or bear
  The avenging sword to smite:
Nor Mercy's ever gladdening eye
Permit the ruffian to defy
  Th' unerring rule of right.

VII.

To Justice, dearer far the part
  To tune the plausive voice;
Of Virtue to delight the heart,
  And bid the good rejoice.

To yield the meed of grateful praise—
The deathless monument to raise,
To honor Virtue dead;
Or wreathe the chaplet of renown,
The laurel or the mural crown,
For living Virtue's head.

VIII.

Here, to defend his native land,
His sword the patriot draws;
Here the mock hero lifts his hand
To aid a tyrant's cause.
When, meeting on the field of blood,
They pour the sanguinary flood,
Whose triumph waves unfurled?
Alas! let Cheronea tell;
Or plains where godlike Brutus fell,
Or Cæsar won the world!

IX.

In arms, when hostile nations rise
And blood the strife decides,
'Tis brutal force awards the prize,
Her head while Justice hides.
But short is force's triumph base:
Justice unveils her awful face,
And hurls him from the steep;
Strips from his brow the wreath of fame,

And after ages load his name
  With curses loud and deep.

X.

Behold the lettered sage devote
  The labors of his mind,
His country's welfare to promote,
  And benefit mankind.
Lo! from the blackest caves of hell,
A phalanx fierce of monsters fell,
  Combine their fearful bands—
His fame asperse, his toils assail;
Till Justice holds aloft her scale
  And shields him from their hands.

XI.

Of excellence, in every clime,
  'Tis thus the lot is cast;
Passion usurps the present time,
  But Justice rules the past:
Envy, and selfishness, and pride,
The passing hours of man divide
  With unresisted sway;
But Justice comes, with noiseless tread,
O'ertakes the filmy spider's thread
  And sweeps the net away.

XII.

Eternal Spirit! Lord supreme
  Of blessing and of woe!

Of Justice, ever living stream!
  Whose mercies ceaseless flow—
Make me, while earth shall be my span,
Just to my fellow-mortal, man,
  Whate'er my lot may be.
And when this transient scene is o'er,
Pure let my deathless spirit soar,
  And Mercy find from thee.

U of M

TO SALLY.

"Integer vitæ, scelerisque purus
Non eget Mauris jaculis, neque arcu."

THE man in righteousness array'd,
A pure and blameless liver,
Needs not the keen Toledo blade,
Nor venom-freighted quiver.
What though he wind his toilsome way
O'er regions wild and weary—
Through Zara's burning desert stray;
Or Asia's jungles dreary:

What though he plough the billowy deep
By lunar light, or solar,
Meet the resistless Simoon's sweep,
Or iceberg circumpolar.
In bog or quagmire deep and dank,
His foot shall never settle;
He mounts the summit of Mont Blanc,
Or Popocatapetl.

On Chimborazo's breathless height,
He treads o'er burning lava;

Or snuffs the Bohan Upas blight,
The deathful plant of Java.
Through every peril he shall pass,
By Virtue's shield protected;
And still by Truth's unerring glass
His path shall be directed.

Else wherefore was it, Thursday last,
While strolling down the valley
Defenceless, musing as I pass'd
A canzonet to Sally;
A wolf, with mouth protruding snout,
Forth from the thicket bounded—
I clapped my hands and raised a shout—
He heard—and fled—confounded.

Tangier nor Tunis never bred
An animal more crabbed;
Nor Fez, dry nurse of lions, fed
A monster half so rabid.
Nor Ararat so fierce a beast
Has seen, since days of Noah;
Nor strong, more eager for a feast,
The fell constrictor boa.

Oh! place me where the solar beam
Has scorch'd all verdure vernal;
Or on the polar verge extreme,
Block'd up with ice eternal—

Still shall my voice's tender lays
  Of love remain unbroken;
And still my charming SALLY praise,
  Sweet smiling, and sweet spoken.

TO E—— B——

OH! wherefore, Lady, was my lot
  Cast from thy own so far?
Why, by kind Fortune, live we not
  Beneath one blessed star?
For, had thy thread of life and mine
  But side by side been spun,
My heart had panted to entwine
  The tissue into ONE.

And why should Time conspire
  To sever us in twain?
And wherefore have I run my race,
  And cannot start again?
Thy thread, how long! how short is mine!
  Mine spent—thine scarce begun:
Alas! we never can entwine
  The tissue into ONE

But, take my blessings on thy name—
  The blessing of a sire;
Not from a lover's furnace flame—
  'Tis from a holier fire:

A thread unseen beside of thine
By fairy forms is spun—
And holy hands shall soon entwine
The tissue into ONE.

TO A LADY

WHO PRESENTED HIM A PAIR OF KNIT GLOVES.

Who shall say that public life
Is nothing but discordant strife?
And he whose heart is tuned to love,
Tender and gentle as the dove,
Must whet his talons, night and day,
For conflicts with the birds of prey?

This world is fashioned, Lady fair,
Of Joy and Sorrow, Ease and Care;
Of sudden changes, small and great;
Of upward and of downward fate:
And whoso bends his mood to trace
The annals of man's fallen race,
May sigh to find that nature's plan
Is ruthless war from man to man.
But nature, cruel to be kind,
Not to war only man consigned;
But gave him woman on the spot,
To mingle pleasure in his lot:
That if with man war cannot cease,
With woman reigns eternal peace.

Fair Lady, I have lived on earth
Nigh fourscore summers from my birth;
And half the sorrows I have felt
Have by my brother man been dealt;
And all the ills I have endured
By man inflicted, woman cured.
The glove from man to man, thou know'st,
Of fierce defiance is the boast;
And cast in anger on the floor,
To mortal combat shows the door:
But gloves from woman's gentle hand,
Of cordial Friendship bear the wand;
And in return a single glove
Betokens emblematic Love.

Thy gift, fair Ellen, then I take,
And cherish for the giver's sake;
And while they shelter from the storm
My hands, the heart alike shall warm;
And speed for thee to God above,
The fervid prayer of faithful love.

THE LIP AND THE HEART.

One day between the Lip and the Heart
  A wordless strife arose,
Which was expertest in the art
  His purpose to disclose.

The Lip called forth the vassal Tongue,
  And made him vouch—a lie!
The slave his servile anthem sung,
  And brav'd the listening sky.

The Heart to speak in vain essay'd,
  Nor could his purpose reach—
His will nor voice nor tongue obeyed,
  His silence was his speech.

Mark thou their difference, child of earth!
  While each performs his part,
Not all the lip can speak is worth
  The silence of the heart.

WRITTEN IN AN ALBUM.

In days of yore, the poet's pen
From wing of bird was plundered;
Perhaps of goose, but, now and then,
From Jove's own eagle sundered.
But now metallic pens disclose
Alone the poet's numbers
In iron inspiration glows,
Or with the minstrel slumbers.

Fair damsel! could my pen impart,
In prose or lofty rhyme,
The pure emotions of my heart,
To speed the flight of time;
What metal from the womb of earth
Could worth intrinsic bear,
To stamp with corresponding worth
The blessings thou shouldst share?

www.ingramcontent.com/pod-product-compliance
Lightning Source LLC
LaVergne TN
LVHW021429110826
845150LV00007B/2151